STEP UP

Engaging math activities, games, and
fact cards PLUS fun math-related stories
to reinforce key math concepts!

Senior Editor: Janet Sweet
Design/Production: Rebekah Lewis
Art Director: Moonhee Pak
Managing Editor: Stacey Faulkner

Table of Contents

MATH Introduction and Glossary 3

MATH Activities. 7

MATH Stories and Companion Activities

The Crayola® Counting Book *story and companion activities* 37

The Ten-Second Race *story and companion activities* 55

Lemonade *story and companion activities* 73

MATH Games 91

MATH Fact Cards 101

MATH Answer Key 121

MATH Award 127

MATH Introduction

Understanding math is vitally important to your child's success in school and in life. The MATH series by Creative Teaching Press is expertly developed to help young children understand math concepts and ideas that relate to their world. Appealing activities and games, along with stories, fact cards, and a helpful glossary, support math success while making math fun.

Positive attitudes about math at home—including yours as a parent—lay the foundation for math success in school. Make a point of helping your child notice math-related activities and concepts that occur in his or her daily world, such as pointing out house numbers or counting cars or noticing clothing sizes. Also encourage your child to try these activities to practice thinking mathematically:

- Sort—clothes, toys
- Measure—ingredients, sizes
- Estimate—distance, time
- Tell—where, when, and how
- Play—card and board games
- Count—stairs, grocery items
- Compare—shapes, sizes, numbers
- Pretend—to be a waiter, cashier

Helping your child experience fun, real-world math interaction at an early age will build math enjoyment, knowledge, and success throughout your child's life.

MATH Glossary

Learning math can be a challenge for young children. At a time when they are just learning to recognize and understand basic words and language skills, young learners must also figure out the symbols, concepts, and specialized vocabulary of math—all of which can seem like an entirely different language.

Specifically designed for First and Second Graders, this  Glossary provides visual examples with clear, easy-to-understand definitions for the important math terms they must learn.

For extra support, these words also appear in red font both here and in the math-related story questions. Calling out math words in this way helps young learners understand that math is a meaningful part of everyday language and does not exist solely on math worksheets.

SYMBOLS AND CONCEPTS

+	addition sign (also called *plus sign*)
–	subtraction sign (also called *minus sign*)
=	equal sign
$	dollar sign
¢	cent sign
>	greater than $5 > 2$
<	less than $1 < 9$

LOCATION AND POSITION WORDS

above		above **the ants**
after	16 17	**17** is after **16**
before	7 8	**7** is before **8**
below	$\frac{1}{2}$	**2** is below **1**
between	23, 24, 25	**24** is between **23** and **25**
next to		The circle is next to **the rectangles.**

MATH+ Step Up • Gr. 1–2 © 2011 Creative Teaching Press

COUNTING, SHAPE, AND MATH-FACT WORDS

add

combine numbers or objects together

$3 + 2 = 5$

half

difference

$9 - 3 = 6 \longleftarrow$ difference

ordinal number

tells the order or sequence

1st   2nd   3rd   4th

equal parts

This shape has 4 equal parts.

shapes

circle   rectangle   square   triangle

cone   cube   cylinder   sphere

estimate

find out <u>about</u> how many or how much

The crayon is about 4 paper clips long.

side

This shape has 4 sides.

fact family

The fact family for numbers 3, 5, and 8 is:

8
3   5
$5 + 3 = 8$
$3 + 5 = 8$
$8 - 5 = 3$
$8 - 3 = 5$

subtract

take away objects from a group

$5 - 3 = 2$

fraction

any part of a whole object

$\frac{1}{2}$ $\frac{1}{3}$

$\frac{1}{2}$ (one half) and $\frac{1}{3}$ (one third) are fractions

sum

$4 + 1 = 5 \longleftarrow$ sum

graphs

Favorite Color

blue
red
0 1 2 3 4 5 6 7 8

bar graph

Favorite Fruits

apples
bananas
grapes

picture graph

tens

2 tens = 20

MATH+ Step Up • Gr. 1–2 © 2011 Creative Teaching Press

TIME, MONEY, AND MEASUREMENT WORDS

a.m. and p.m.	Midnight Midday Midnight a.m. p.m.	**inch**	0 1 2 3 4 5
cup		**minute**	1:00 1:01 1 minute = 60 seconds
dime	10¢ or 10 cents = 10 pennies	**nickel**	5¢ or 5 cents = 5 pennies
dollar	$1.00 or one dollar = 100 pennies	**penny**	1¢ or 1 cent
foot	1 foot = 12 inches	**pint**	1 pint = 2 cups
gallon	1 gallon = 4 quarts or 8 pints or 16 cups	**quart**	1 quart = 2 pints or 4 cups
half dollar	50¢ or 50 cents = 50 pennies	**quarter**	25¢ or 25 cents = 25 pennies
half hour	A half hour is 30 minutes.	**second**	a measure of time 60 seconds = 1 minute
hour	An hour is 60 minutes.	**temperature**	how hot or cold

MATH+ Step Up • Gr. 1–2 © 2011 Creative Teaching Press

Caterpillar Counting

- Look at each pattern.
- Write the missing numbers.

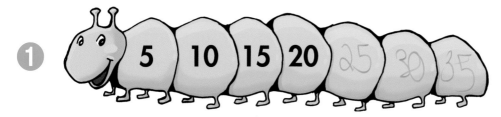

1 5 10 15 20 25 30 35

What is the pattern? _____

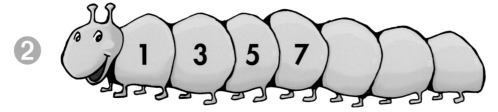

2 1 3 5 7

What is the pattern? _____

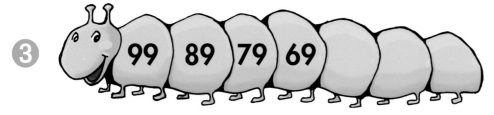

3 99 89 79 69

What is the pattern? _____

4 4 8 12 16

What is the pattern? _____

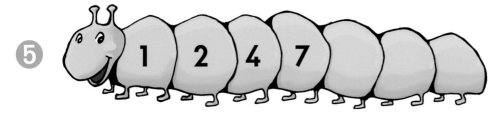

5 1 2 4 7

What is the pattern? _____

Number Riddles

○ Solve the number riddles.

○ Circle the correct answers.

1 I have 1 ten and 6 ones.
What number am I?

61   16

2 I have 3 tens and 2 ones.
What number am I?

32   23

3 I have 9 ones and less
than 4 tens.
What number am I?

49   29

4 I have 2 ones and more
than 6 tens.
What number am I?

72   52

5 I have 8 tens and more
than 7 ones.
What number am I?

89   86

6 I have 4 tens and less
than 5 ones.
What number am I?

47   43

7 I have less than 7 ones
and more than 5 tens.
What number am I?

55   61

8 I have more than 3 ones
and less than 7 tens.
What number am I?

88   56

9 I have less than 5 tens
and more than 4 ones.
What number am I?

54   45

10 I have more than 6 tens
and less than 5 ones.
What number am I?

33   91

MATH+ Step Up • Gr. 1–2 © 2011 Creative Teaching Press

Mystery Numbers

⚙ Look at the numbers in each set.

⚙ Use them to write numbers that match the clues.

⚙ Do not use a number more than once for each set.

1 The number is even.
It is greater than 35.
It is less than 50.

5
2
6
_____
3

2 The number is odd.
It is greater than 85.
It is less than 90.

9
8
2
_____
5

3 The number is even.
It is greater than 60.
It is less than 70.

3
7
6
_____
2

4 The number is even.
It is greater than 60.
It is less than 70.

4
6
7
_____
9

5 The number is even.
It is greater than 25.
It is less than 30.

2
8
4
_____
3

6 The number is odd.
It is greater than 80.
It is less than 95.

1
9
7
_____
4

7 The number is odd.
It is greater than 45.
It is less than 75.

3
9
4
_____
2

8 The number is even.
It is greater than 13.
It is less than 21.

8
2
3
_____
1

What's Half?

☼ Color the pictures to match the fractions.

1 Color $\frac{1}{2}$ of the bananas.

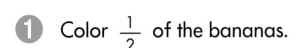

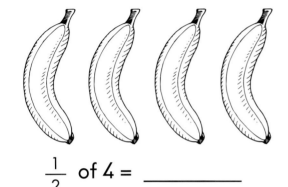

$\frac{1}{2}$ of 4 = _____

2 Color $\frac{1}{2}$ of the oranges.

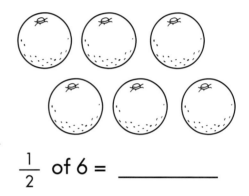

$\frac{1}{2}$ of 6 = _____

3 Color $\frac{1}{2}$ of the cherries.

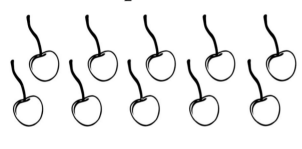

$\frac{1}{2}$ of 10 = _____

4 Color $\frac{1}{2}$ of the apples.

$\frac{1}{2}$ of 8 = _____

5 Color $\frac{1}{2}$ of the pineapples.

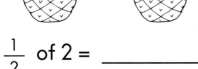

$\frac{1}{2}$ of 2 = _____

6 Color $\frac{1}{2}$ of the strawberries.

$\frac{1}{2}$ of 12 = _____

MATH⁺ Step Up • Gr. 1–2 © 2011 Creative Teaching Press

Addition Detective

- Look at the numbers in the box.
- Circle three numbers in a row that add up to 12.
- The numbers can go **across** or **down**.
- When you are finished, 12 sets of numbers should be circled.
- The first one is done for you.

    Hint: A number can be used in more than one problem.

4	5	8	3	2	7	9
6	9	5	1	6	3	2
2	3	3	6	5	3	2
3	5	4	8	2	4	8
8	1	2	9	5	5	6
1	9	5	7	1	4	5

Something Fishy

- Help the shark catch the fish!
- Follow the path from the shark to each fish, subtracting the numbers from 13.
- Write the final answer on each fish.

MATH+ Step Up • Gr. 1–2 © 2011 Creative Teaching Press

Spider Web

○ Cut out the number squares at the bottom of the page.

○ Place the numbers in the spider web so that the sum of each row is 17.

○ One number will be left over. What is it? _____

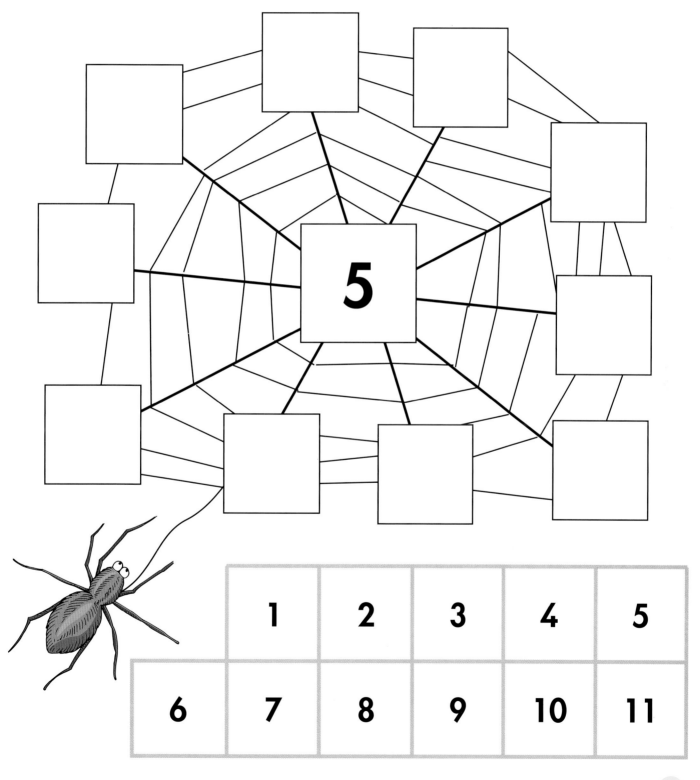

1	2	3	4	5
6	7	8	9	10	11

Hocus, Pocus!

☼ Help the wizard make three-digit numbers.

☼ Use the digits on each set of stars to write each number.

1 largest three-digit number _____

2 smallest three-digit number _____

3 largest three-digit number
with the 9 in the tens place _____

4 largest three-digit number _____

5 smallest three-digit number _____

6 largest three-digit number
with the 6 in the ones place _____

7 largest three-digit number _____

8 smallest three-digit number _____

9 largest three-digit number
with the 7 in the ones place _____

Secret Subtraction

- There are 13 subtraction problems in this puzzle. The first one is done for you.

- Circle the other 12 problems.

- They can go **across** or **down**.

  Hint: A number can be used in more than one problem.

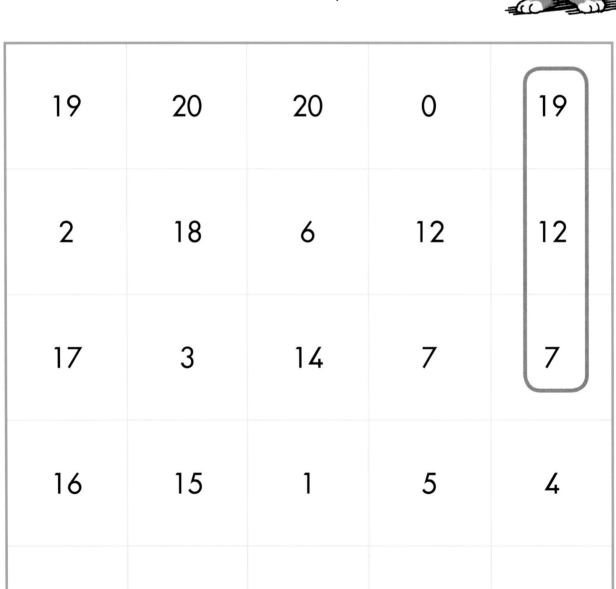

19	20	20	0	19
2	18	6	12	12
17	3	14	7	7
16	15	1	5	4
11	7	4	2	3

MATH⁺ Step Up • Gr. 1–2 © 2011 Creative Teaching Press

Plus and Minus Puzzler

☼ Look at each row of numbers.

☼ Write + or − in the circles to make two number sentences that are equal.

1 3 ◯ 5 = 9 ◯ 1

2 11 ◯ 4 = 12 ◯ 5

3 6 ◯ 4 = 8 ◯ 6

4 8 ◯ 5 = 7 ◯ 6

5 10 ◯ 5 = 2 ◯ 3

6 5 ◯ 3 = 10 ◯ 2

7 6 ◯ 6 = 9 ◯ 3

8 13 ◯ 5 = 6 ◯ 2

9 11 ◯ 2 = 3 ◯ 6

10 10 ◯ 6 = 12 ◯ 8

11 7 ◯ 3 = 2 ◯ 8

12 12 ◯ 3 = 4 ◯ 5

Play Ball!

- Subtract the numbers in each problem.

- Then circle the letters that belong to answers of 8 or less.

- Starting at the arrow, write the letters you circled in order on the lines below. The first one is done for you.

Riddle: How did the player know the baseball was laughing?

Answer:

IT WAS _I_ ___ ___ ___ ___ ___ ___ ___ ___ ___.

MATH+ Step Up • Gr. 1–2 © 2011 Creative Teaching Press

Picnic Guest

- Help Adam Ant take three different paths to the picnic basket.
- Begin at each arrow and draw the path with a pencil.
- Then start with 19 and subtract the numbers along each path.
- Write your answers in the circles.

A Space Trip

Help the alien get to his planet.

Solve each problem on the path.

① 362
  +125

② 214
  + 54

③ 689
  +127

④ 300
  +600

⑤ 861
  +140

⑥ 783
  + 23

⑦ 415
  + 34

⑧ 278
  + 78

⑨ 64
  + 123

⑩ 704
  +210

⑪ 512
  +367

⑫ 437
  + 36

⑬ 620
  +510

⑭ 700
  + 500

⑮ 102
  +297

⑯ 415
  +380

⑰ 936
  +630

⑱ 615
  +605

MATH+ Step Up • Gr. 1–2 © 2011 Creative Teaching Press

Passing the Time

- ☼ Solve each problem.
- ☼ Write the time.
- ☼ Then draw hands on the clock to match.

1 The movie started at 3:00. It lasted 2 hours. What time did the movie end?

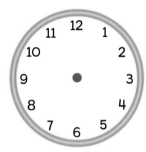

_____

2 Meg went to Kim's house at 11:30. She stayed for 3 hours. What time did Meg leave?

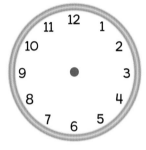

_____

3 Lynn sleeps for 9 hours each night. She goes to bed at 9:00. What time does she get up?

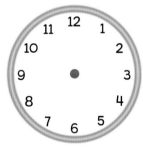

_____

4 Matt read for half an hour. He finished at 7:45. What time did Matt start reading?

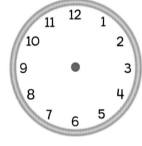

_____

5 Mr. Mays left home at 10:30. He returned 5 hours later. What time did he get home?

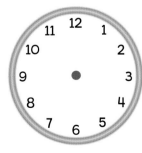

_____

6 Mrs. Lum shopped for half an hour. She finished at 2:15. What time did she start shopping?

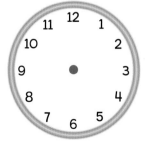

_____

Time Puzzlers

Solve these time puzzlers.

1 Neil has a baseball game at 3:00. It will take him half an hour to get to the park. What time does Neil have to leave home to get to the park by 3:00?

_____

2 Wendy's school starts at 8:30. It takes her 15 minutes to walk to school. What is the latest time that Wendy can leave home?

_____

3 A movie ended at 8:00. It lasted $2\frac{1}{2}$ hours. What time did the movie start?

_____

4 Kenny gets up every morning at 7:00. He always has 10 hours of sleep. What time does Kenny go to bed?

_____

5 Jessica shopped for 1 hour and 15 minutes. She finished at 4:15. What time did Jessica start shopping?

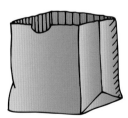

_____

6 Mickey met his grandmother at 1:45. His visit lasted $3\frac{1}{2}$ hours. What time did he leave his grandmother?

_____

MATH⁺ Step Up • Gr. 1–2 © 2011 Creative Teaching Press

Matching Coin Sets

☸ Draw a line from each coin purse to the wallet that has the same amount of money.

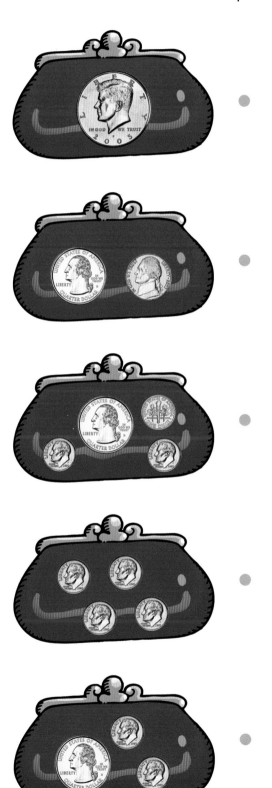

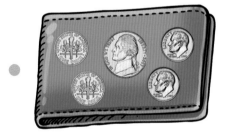

Money Match

Fill in the bubble to show the correct answer.

1 How much is this?

37¢ 60¢ 62¢
○   ○   ○

2 How much is this?

40¢ 51¢ 61¢
○   ○   ○

3 How much is [$10 bill] worth?

$10 $1 $5
○   ○   ○

4 How much is this?

$6.28 $10.00 $10.28
○   ○   ○

5 How much is this?

$3.24
+$4.12

$7.36 $7.32 $1.12
○   ○   ○

6 Bob has 34¢. He spends 22¢ on [candy].

How much money is left?

46¢ 22¢ 12¢
○   ○   ○

MATH+ Step Up • Gr. 1–2 © 2011 Creative Teaching Press

At the Fair

- Look at the price of each item.
- Then solve the problems.

| flag | balloon | ice cream | monkey | clown |

1 David has 2 dimes. What can he buy?

_____

2 Elsie has 5 dimes. How many flags can she buy?

_____

3 Jenna has 2 quarters. What is the most expensive item she can buy?

_____

4 Marcus has 3 quarters. What is the most expensive thing he can buy?

_____

5 Paul has 2 quarters and 1 dime. How much more money does he need to buy the clown?

_____

6 Jessica has 2 quarters and 2 nickels. How much more money does she need to buy the monkey?

_____

7 Kim has 3 quarters. How many balloons can she buy?

_____

8 Matt has 3 quarters and 2 dimes. He wants to buy 3 different items. What can he buy?

_____

At the Toy Store

⚙ Look at the prices of the toys.

⚙ Then solve the problems.

Top	$1.15	Ball	$1.25
Car	$2.25	Yo-Yo	$1.00
Bear	$3.00	Drum	$2.50

1 Mandy bought two different toys. She spent $4.00. What did she buy?

_____

2 Brian bought two different toys. He spent $3.65. What did he buy?

_____

3 Sara and Kyle each bought a toy. Sara's toy cost 15¢ more than Kyle's toy. What did each child buy?

Sara _____   Kyle _____

4 Nikki and Brandon each bought a toy. Nikki's toy cost $1.00 less than Brandon's toy. What did each child buy?

Nikki _____   Brandon _____

5 Scott has $3.00. He will buy two different toys. What are the two most expensive toys he can buy?

_____

MATH+ Step Up • Gr. 1–2 © 2011 Creative Teaching Press

Change, Please!

☼ Answer each question with the correct amount of change.

Megan has $1.00

1 If Megan buys a

50¢

how much change
will she get? _____

2 If she buys a

75¢

how much change
will she get? _____

3 If she buys a

$1.00

how much change
will she get? _____

4 If she buys a

25¢

how much change
will she get? _____

5 If she buys a

60¢

how much change
will she get? _____

6 If she buys a

45¢

how much change
will she get? _____

7 If she buys a

15¢

how much change
will she get? _____

8 If she buys a

30¢

how much change
will she get? _____

Lunchtime

○ Use the menu to help you find out the cost of each lunch.

○ Then write how much change each child received.

MENU

Apple 30¢	Hot Dog $1.35	French Fries 80¢
Banana 25¢	Sandwich $1.95	Milk 45¢
	Hamburger $2.25	

1 Mia had $3.00. She bought a sandwich and milk.

cost _____   change _____

2 Kevin had $4.00. He bought a hamburger and french fries.

cost _____   change _____

3 Carly had $1.00. She bought an apple and two bananas.

cost _____   change _____

4 Devon had $2.75. He bought two hot dogs.

cost _____   change _____

5 Jacob had $5.00. He bought a hamburger, a hot dog, and french fries.

cost _____   change _____

MATH⁺ Step Up • Gr. 1–2 © 2011 Creative Teaching Press

How Much?

Answer each problem with the correct unit of measure.

2 cups	=	1 pint
2 pints	=	1 quart
4 quarts	=	1 gallon

1. Sara is having some soup. Will she drink about 1 cup or 1 quart of soup?

_____

2. Kent is making some pudding. He needs 3 cups of milk. Should he buy 1 pint or 1 quart of milk?

_____

3. Lauren has invited 8 friends to her home. She will make some juice for them. Will she need 1 quart or 1 gallon of juice?

_____

4. Evan poured some lemonade for himself and a friend. Did he pour about 1 pint or 1 quart of lemonade in all?

_____

5. Mrs. Lee made a pot of soup for her family. Did she make about 1 pint or 1 gallon of soup?

_____

Equal Measures

Fill in the blanks.

 =  = 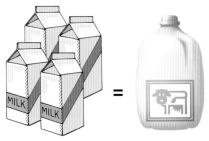 =

2 cups = 1 pint   **2 pints = 1 quart**   **4 quarts = 1 gallon**

1

1 pint = _____ cups

2 pints = _____ cups

3 pints = _____ cups

4 pints = _____ cups

2

1 quart = _____ pints

1 quart = _____ cups

2 quarts = _____ pints

2 quarts = _____ cups

3

1 gallon = _____ quarts

2 gallons = _____ quarts

3 gallons = _____ quarts

4 gallons = _____ quarts

4

1 gallon = _____ pints

1 gallon = _____ cups

2 gallons = _____ pints

2 gallons = _____ cups

MATH+ Step Up • Gr. 1–2 © 2011 Creative Teaching Press

Zoo Animals

✿ Cindy kept track of the animals she saw at the zoo.

✿ Use the graph to answer the questions below.

✿ = 2 animals

zebra	✿ ✿
monkey	✿ ✿ ✿ ✿ ✿ ✿
snake	✿ ✿ ✿ ✿
hippo	✿ ✿ ✿
penguin	✿ ✿ ✿ ✿ ✿

1 How many zebras did Cindy see? _____

2 How many monkeys did Cindy see? _____

3 Were there more penguins or snakes? _____

4 How many hippos and zebras were there altogether? _____

5 How many more monkeys were there than snakes _____

6 How many more hippos were there than zebras? _____

Classroom Contest

✿ This graph shows how much money the second grade made by selling carnival tickets for a nickel each.

✿ Use the graph to answer the questions below.

Carnival Ticket Sales

$2.50				
$2.25				
$2.00				
$1.75				
$1.50				
$1.25				
$1.00				
75¢				
50¢				
25¢				
	Room 1	Room 2	Room 3	Room 4

1 How much did Room 1 make? _____

2 How much did Room 3 make? _____

3 Which room made the most money? _____

4 How much was it? _____

5 Which room made the least money? _____

6 How much was it? _____

7 How much more money did Room 4 make than Room 1? _____

8 How much money did Rooms 1 and 3 make altogether? _____

MATH+ Step Up • Gr. 1–2 © 2011 Creative Teaching Press

What's the Magic Rule?

⚙ Look at each number going in and the number coming out.

⚙ Solve the magic rule that was used to change the number.

⚙ Fill in the rest of the missing numbers using the magic rule. Then write the rule in the bottom of the box.

⚙ The first one is done for you.

IN	OUT
10	11
12	13
14	15
16	17
18	19
20	21
Rule: +1	

IN	OUT
18	15
12	9
10	
16	
20	
15	
Rule:	

IN	OUT
5	10
6	12
7	
8	
9	
10	
Rule:	

IN	OUT
5	10
12	17
8	
10	
14	
20	
Rule:	

IN	OUT
10	8
2	0
6	
8	
4	
3	
Rule:	

IN	OUT
12	6
10	4
16	
14	
11	
18	
Rule:	

Who's Who?

⚙ Read the clues.

⚙ Then write each child's name under the correct picture.

1 Clues:
- Sid is taller than Jim.
- Tom is taller than Jim.
- Sid is taller than Tom.

_____ _____ _____

2 Clues:
- Sue is taller than Dee.
- Bev is taller than Jan.
- Jan is taller than Sue.

_____ _____ _____ _____

MATH+ Step Up • Gr. 1–2 © 2011 Creative Teaching Press

All in the Family

✿ Solve the problems to find out everyone's age.

1 Jim is 3 years older than his sister Kim.
Their ages add up to 13.

How old is Jim? _____

How old is Kim? _____

2 Sandy and Mandy are twins.
In two years, their ages will add up to 18.

How old are the twins today? _____

3 Meg's mom is twice as old as Meg.
Together, their ages add up to 60.

How old is Meg? _____

How old is Meg's mom? _____

4 Cory's dad is three times as old as Cory.
Cory's grandfather is two times the age
of Corey's dad.
The ages of Cory, his dad, and his
grandfather add up to 100.

How old is Cory? _____

How old is Cory's dad? _____

How old is Cory's grandfather? _____

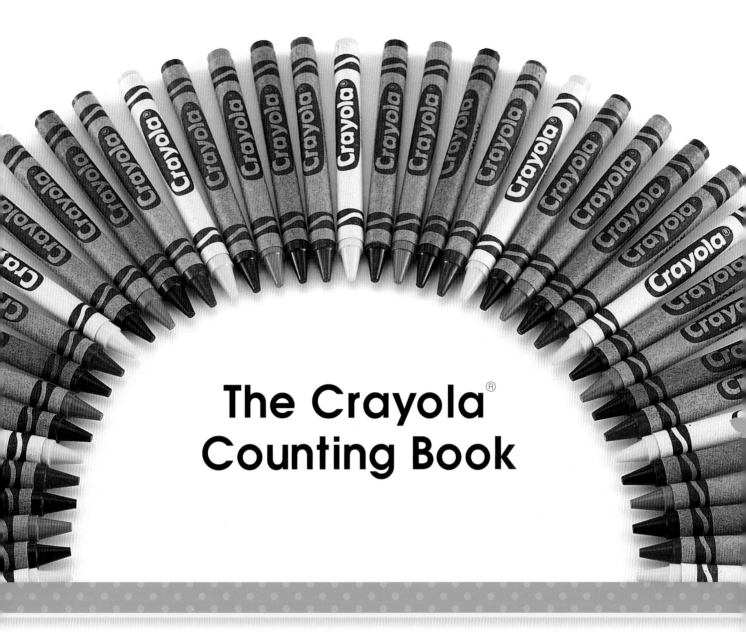

The Crayola® Counting Book

☼ Starting with yellow, what is the color pattern of the crayons above?

☼ How many complete sets of that pattern do you count?

Open the box.
The crayons fall out.

☼ There are 10 crayons in the box and 3 loose crayons.

☼ How would you write this as an addition fact?

MATH⁺ Step Up • Gr. 1–2 © 2011 Creative Teaching Press

Counting crayons
is what it's about!

⚙ The boy is holding 12 crayons in one hand and 13 crayons in the other hand.

⚙ Use numbers and symbols to write that 12 is less than 13.

Count the red crayons.
Count the blues.

☀ How many pairs of red and blue crayons do you count?

☀ If you subtract 3 pairs, how many would be left?

MATH+ Step Up • Gr. 1–2 © 2011 Creative Teaching Press

Count by fives.
Count by twos.

⚙ Add the sets of 5 to the sets of 2.

⚙ How many sets are there altogether?

⚙ How many crayons are there altogether?

Count the crayons
in the smallest pack.

☼ How many more crayons are in the 2nd pack than in the 1st pack?

☼ How many more crayons are in the 3rd pack than in the 1st pack?

MATH+ Step Up • Gr. 1–2 © 2011 Creative Teaching Press

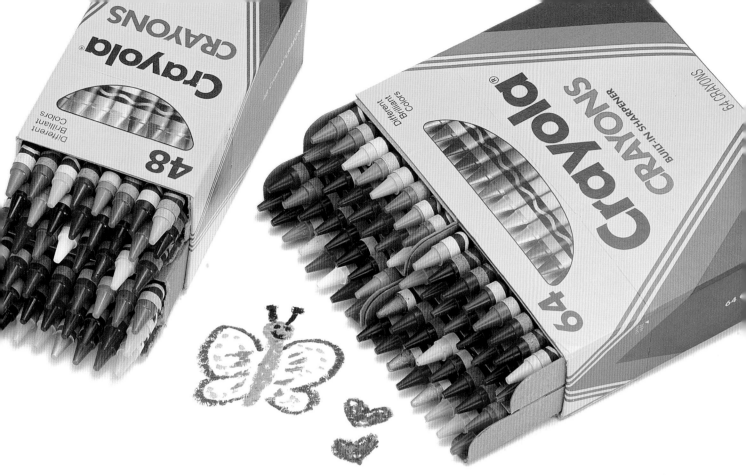

Now count the crayons
in the biggest pack.

⚙ Look at the 2 packs above.

⚙ How many more crayons are in
the 64-crayon pack than the
48-crayon pack?

⚙ How would you write that as a
subtraction fact?

Count the orange crayons.
Count the brown.

- ✦ The number of orange crayons is equal to the number of brown crayons.

- ✦ Let's say that there were 16 more orange crayons.

- ✦ Use numbers and symbols to write that there are more orange crayons than brown crayons.

**Count the ones
that fell on the ground.**

- ☼ There are 2 green crayons in the group above.
- ☼ Compare that with the number of crayons on this page altogether.
- ☼ How would you write that as a fraction?

Count the crayons.
Count by tens.

☀ How many sets of 10 crayons would you
need to subtract on this page to equal
40 crayons altogether?

Did you count one hundred?
Count them again!

☼ Look at both this page and page 46.

☼ How many sets of 10 crayons would you need to add to equal 120 crayons altogether?

**Crayons can be counted.
Counting is great!**

☼ Would you estimate that there are more than 50 crayons or less than 50 crayons above?

☼ Look closely. What do you see that tells you the kids above are counting by 5s?

MATH+ Step Up • Gr. 1–2 © 2011 Creative Teaching Press

But the best thing about crayons . . .

- ☼ Add the loose crayons above to the crayons in the yellow and green Crayola® box.

- ☼ How would you write that as an addition fact?

- ☼ Now also add the 7 crayons in the red pouch. How many crayons do you count altogether?

is the pictures you make!

✸ Count the number of kids in the group above.

✸ How would you write the fraction that compares the number of girls to this group?

MATH+ Step Up • Gr. 1–2 © 2011 Creative Teaching Press

It's fun to draw and color, too.

☼ How would you write the fraction that compares the number of boys to the number of kids in the group above?

☼ Is this fraction greater than or less than the fraction on page 50?

Now let's see what you can do!

⚙ Count the number of picture drawings above.

⚙ How would you write the fraction that compares the number of faces without a nose to the group?

MATH⁺ Step Up • Gr. 1–2 © 2011 Creative Teaching Press

Make a Mini Book

- ✪ Cut along the <u>solid</u> lines.
- ✪ Fold on the <u>dotted</u> lines and staple.
- ✪ Read and count!

I Can Count

Count the candy.

Count the cats
and the kittens, too.

4

Count the cows that go,
"Moo, moo."

5

Count the kids
and kites you see.

8

I Can Count

Count the candy.

1

Make a Mini Book

Count the kings.

6

Count the cookies
we can make.

3

Count the cakes.

2

Count the keys.

7

MATH+ Step Up • Gr. 1–2 © 2011 Creative Teaching Press

The Ten-Second Race

☼ Compare a stopwatch to a clock.

☼ How are they the same?

☼ How are they different?

The snail, the ant, the mouse, the dog, the horse, and the cheetah are ready!

How many animals are going to race?

Why are the animals wearing numbers?

MATH⁺ Step Up • Gr. 1–2 © 2011 Creative Teaching Press

One, two, three, four, five,
six, seven, eight, nine, ten!
Who will win the ten-second race?

☼ Why is this stopwatch perfect to use
for a ten-second race?

The snail went one inch.

☼ What do you know about snails that explains why this snail went only one inch?

MATH⁺ Step Up • Gr. 1–2 © 2011 Creative Teaching Press

The snail didn't win. Who will win?

☼ How many animals are still in the race?

The ant went one foot.

How many inches did the ant run?

The ant didn't win. Who will win?

⚙ How many animals are still in the race now?

⚙ How would you write this as a subtraction fact?

The mouse went twenty feet.

☼ How many more feet did the mouse run than the ant?

MATH+ Step Up • Gr. 1–2 © 2011 Creative Teaching Press

The mouse didn't win. Who will win?

☼ Which racing numbers so far will not win the race?

☼ Look back at page 56.

☼ Which racing number do you see that could still win the race?

The dog went one hundred yards.

☼ How many feet are in a yard?

☼ Let's say you wanted to figure out how many feet are in 100 yards.

☼ How could you use addition to get the answer?

MATH⁺ Step Up • Gr. 1–2 © 2011 Creative Teaching Press

The dog didn't win. Who will win?

☼ Which animals are still in the race?

The horse went two hundred yards.

☼ How many more yards did the horse run than the dog?

MATH+ Step Up • Gr. 1–2 © 2011 Creative Teaching Press

The horse didn't win. The winner is . . .

☼ Compare how far the dog ran with how far the horse ran.

☼ Which phrase below tells how they compare?

less than half　　half　　more than half

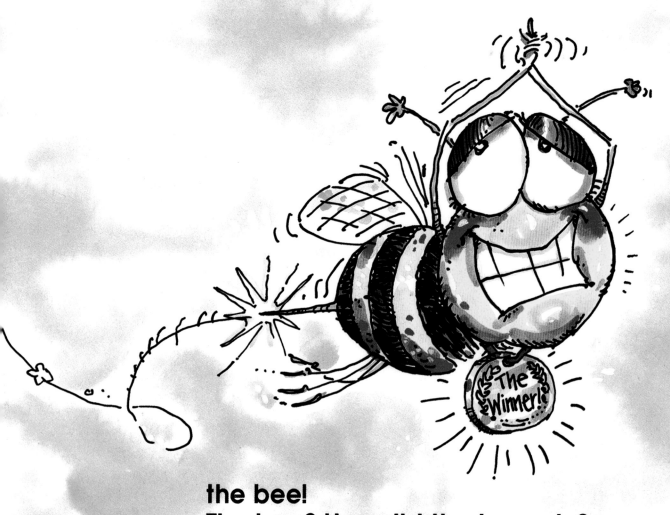

the bee!
The bee? How did the bee win?

☀ Look closely at this page and the next page.

☀ What happened before the cheetah crossed the finish line?

MATH+ Step Up • Gr. 1–2 © 2011 Creative Teaching Press

⚙ Would the cheetah probably have crossed the finish line in 10 seconds or less?

⚙ Explain how you got your answer.

⚙ Did the bee and the cheetah get to the finish line about the same time?

⚙ Do you think it is fair that the bee won the race? Explain your answer.

MATH+ Step Up • Gr. 1–2 © 2011 Creative Teaching Press

How Far Did They Run?

✪ Write the correct letter in each box to answer each question.

I ran 1 inch. Who am I? ☐

I ran 20 feet. Who am I? ☐

I ran 100 yards. Who am I? ☐

I ran 200 yards. Who am I? ☐

Only Inches

○ Help the worm get to the watermelon.

○ Make a path by circling the pictures that are measured in inches.

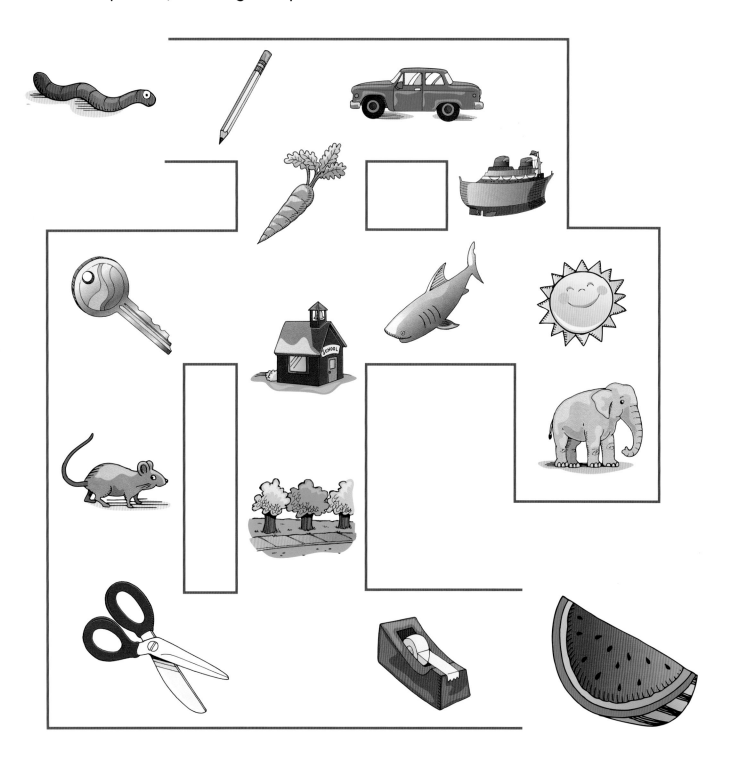

MATH+ Step Up • Gr. 1–2 © 2011 Creative Teaching Press

Lemonade

- ⚙ Look at the containers on the table.
- ⚙ What do you think this story will be about?

It's so hot today.
I could drink a gallon of lemonade.

⚙ Look closely.

⚙ How else could the frog cool off?

MATH+ Step Up • Gr. 1–2 © 2011 Creative Teaching Press

I could drink it all by myself!

☀ Would you probably drink a gallon of lemonade by yourself?

**Here comes my friend.
I will share my lemonade with her.**

☼ Look at page 77.

☼ Once the half gallon jars are filled, how much lemonade will be left in the gallon jar?

MATH+ Step Up • Gr. 1–2 © 2011 Creative Teaching Press

We can each have a half gallon of lemonade.

⚙ Let's say that his jar holds $1\frac{1}{2}$ gallons of lemonade, which he wants to share equally with 2 friends.

⚙ How many half gallon jars would he need altogether?

Here come two more friends.
We can share our lemonade with them.

☼ Finish this math fact:

1 gallon = _____ half gallons

MATH⁺ Step Up • Gr. 1–2 © 2011 Creative Teaching Press

We can each have a quart of lemonade.

✺ How many more quart jars are there than half gallon jars?

✺ How many quart jars equal a gallon jar?

**Here come four more friends.
We can share our lemonade with them, too.**

☼ Compare the number of quart jars to the number of frogs.

☼ How would you write that as a fraction?

MATH+ Step Up • Gr. 1–2 © 2011 Creative Teaching Press

We can each have a pint of lemonade.

⚙ Now compare the number of pint jars to the number of frogs.

⚙ How would you write that as a fraction?

Here come eight more friends.
We can share our lemonade with them, too.

☼ Compare the number of frogs there are now to the number of pint jars on the table.

☼ If every frog got a pint jar, how many more pint jars of lemonade would they need?

MATH⁺ Step Up • Gr. 1–2 © 2011 Creative Teaching Press

We can each have a cup of lemonade.

☼ Compare the number of cup jars above to the number of pint jars on page 82.

☼ How many cups are in a pint?

Wait! I have an idea!

☼ Now compare the number of cup jars on page 83 to the number of quart jars on page 80.

☼ How many cups are in a quart?

MATH+ Step Up • Gr. 1–2 © 2011 Creative Teaching Press

**It's so hot today.
Let's go swimming first!**

- There are 2 pints in a quart, and there are 4 quarts in a gallon.
- How could you use addition to figure out how many pints are in a gallon?

I'll pour the sixteen cups back into the gallon jar.

☼ When he pours half of those cups into the gallon jar, how much will it be?

MATH⁺ Step Up • Gr. 1–2 © 2011 Creative Teaching Press

I'll keep it cold while we swim.

⚙ Finish this math fact:

1 gallon = _____ cups

**How about that!
We still have a gallon of lemonade!**

⚙ Look at the blueberry yogurt container in the refrigerator.

⚙ Compare it with the jars sitting next to the refrigerator.

⚙ Which jar do you estimate would hold less than the yogurt container?

MATH⁺ Step Up • Gr. 1–2 © 2011 Creative Teaching Press

Make a Mini Book

☼ Cut along the <u>solid</u> lines.

☼ Fold on the <u>dotted</u> lines and staple.

☼ Read your book!

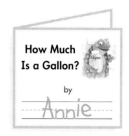

How Much
Is a Gallon?

by

Annie

3

A gallon is 4 quarts.

2

A gallon is 2 half gallons.

A gallon is 8 pints.

4

How Much Is a Gallon?

by

_____

_____

1

Predicting Time Game

HOW TO PLAY

MATERIALS
- ✓ scissors
- ✓ *Predicting Time* game board & game cards

1. Cut apart the game board.

2. Cut apart the clock cards on this page and page 93. Shuffle them and place them facedown in a pile.

3. **Player A**: Pick a card from the pile and put it faceup on the center box of the game board. Read aloud the time shown and what time of day it is.

4. **Player B**: Predict whether the clock card you will pick next will show an earlier time or a later time than the card in the center box. If you think it will be earlier, pick a clock card and put it faceup in the top box. If you think it will be later, pick a clock card and put it faceup in the bottom box.

5. A correct prediction earns **Player B** 2 points. An incorrect prediction earns **Player A** 2 points. Play until a player scores 10 points.

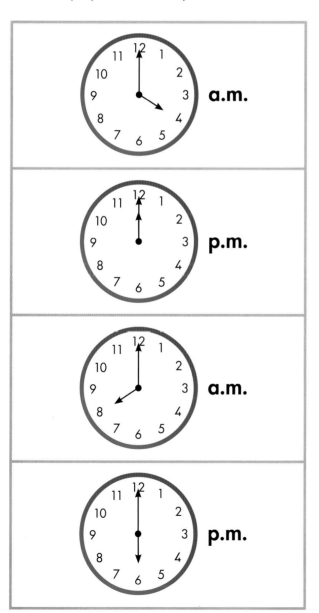

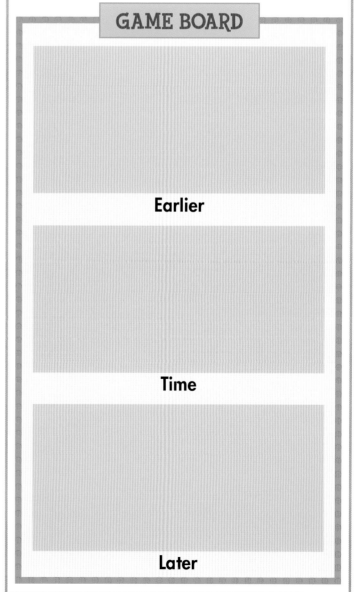

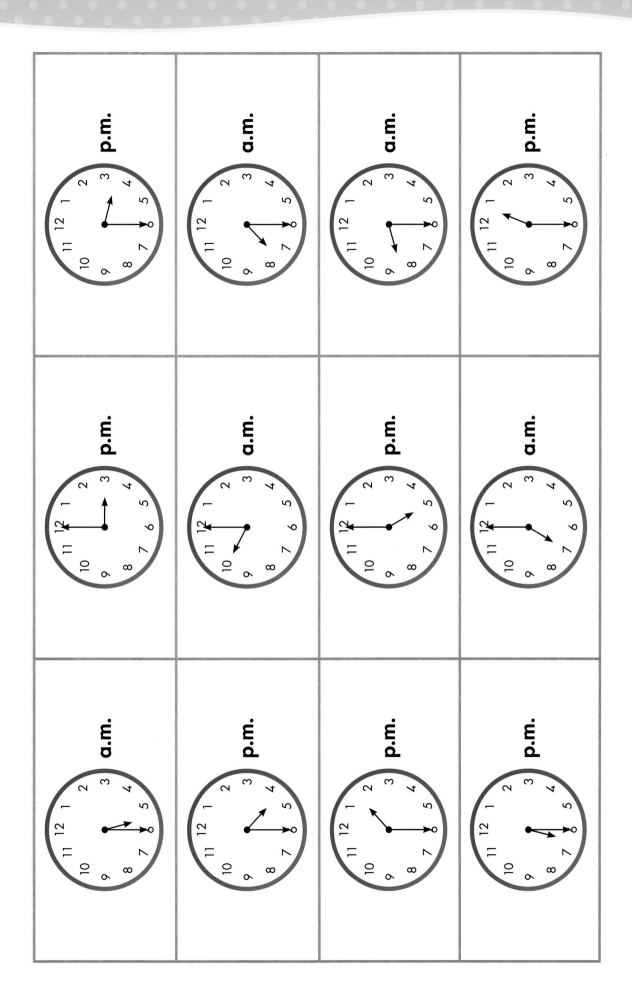

Cover Up Game
Greater Than, Less Than, Equal

HOW TO PLAY

MATERIALS
- ✓ scissors
- ✓ *Cover Up* game board & cards
- ✓ 1 die
- ✓ 2 sets of 13 markers

1. Cut apart the game cards below. Shuffle them and place them facedown in a pile.

2. **Player A**: Roll the die and turn over a card from the pile. Then cover up any number on the board that is less than, greater than, or equal to the number you rolled. For example, if you roll a 4 and turn over the "less than" sign (<), you can cover any number lower than a 4. If you roll a 6 and turn over the "greater than" sign (>), you can cover any number higher than a 6. If you roll a 5 and turn over the "equal" sign (=), you can cover only the 5.

3. **Player B**: Take your turn. If a number has already been covered, you must either make another choice if possible or skip your turn.

4. The first player to cover up a row, a column, or a diagonal line wins.

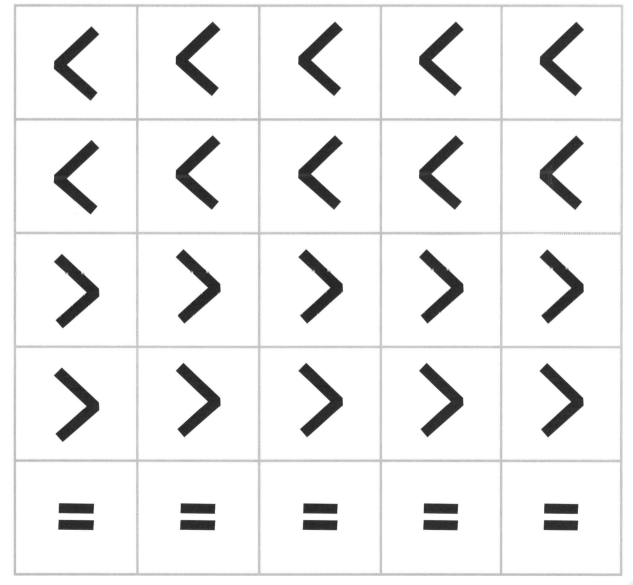

Cover Up Game

Greater Than, Less Than, Equal

1	2	3	4	5
6	7	8	9	10
11	12	13	14	15
16	17	18	19	20
21	22	23	24	25

Tic-Tac-Toe Game

HOW TO PLAY

MATERIALS
- ✓ scissors
- ✓ pencils
- ✓ *Tic-Tac-Bingo* game board
- ✓ MATH+ fact cards (pages 111–117)

1. Cut apart the MATH+ fact cards on pages 103–117. Shuffle them and place them facedown in a pile.

2. **Player A**: Flip over a fact card and solve the problem. Write the answer on any square on the game board.

3. **Player B**: Take your turn doing the same thing.

4. Players continue flipping cards and writing the answers. The goal is to make 3 even-numbered answers appear in a row horizontally, vertically, or diagonally.

5. The first player to get <u>any</u> 3 even-numbered answers in a row wins. If neither player can do this, a new game begins.

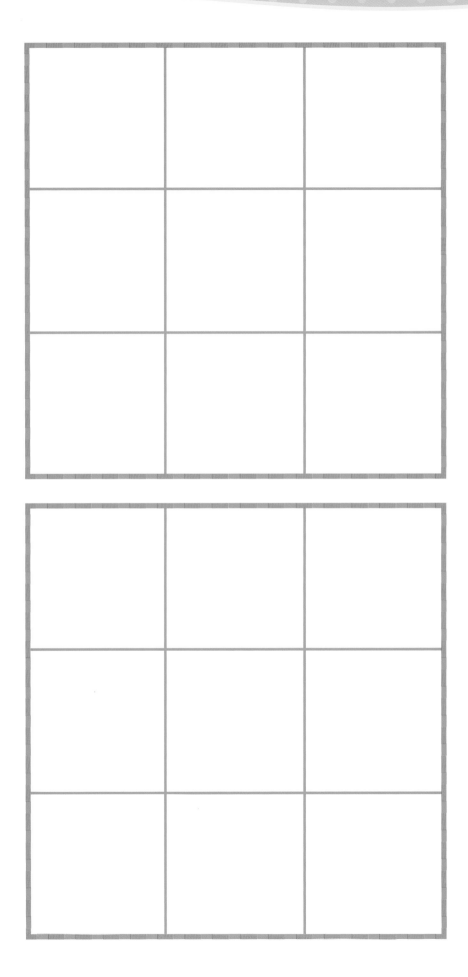

MATH Fact Cards

Tips for Using MATH Fact Cards

Before cutting the fact cards apart, consider laminating them in order to use them with a dry-erase marker. Laminating the cards also makes them more durable. Punching a hole in the upper left-hand corner of each card and storing the cards on a ring is also a good way to keep the cards organized and easy to use.

Here are some suggestions for using the fact cards:

- Use a timer to see how quickly each math fact is recognized. Begin with a small number of cards. Add more cards once your child achieves increased speed and confidence.

- Challenge your child to restate the math fact in another way. For example, 11:30 can be restated as half past eleven.

- Have your child identify the complete fact family for a particular equation. For example, $2 + 3 = 5$ is part of the following fact family: $3 + 2 = 5$, $5 - 3 = 2$, and $5 - 2 = 3$.

- Play a sorting game. Have your child sort the answers to the addition fact cards on pages 103–111 into groups of even and odd numbers. Another option is to shuffle the addition fact cards and sort their answers into groups of 1–10 and 11–20. Alternatively, shuffle the subtraction fact cards on pages 111–119 and sort their answers into groups of 1–4 and 5–9.

The Properties of Zero (0)

When adding zero to a number, the number stays the same.

$1 + 0 = 1$	$2 + 0 = 2$
$3 + 0 = 3$	$4 + 0 = 4$
$5 + 0 = 5$	$6 + 0 = 6$
$7 + 0 = 7$	$8 + 0 = 8$
$9 + 0 = 9$	$10 + 0 = 10$

When subtracting zero from a number, the number stays the same.

1 – 0 = 1	2 – 0 = 2
3 – 0 = 3	4 – 0 = 4
5 – 0 = 5	6 – 0 = 6
7 – 0 = 7	8 – 0 = 8
9 – 0 = 9	10 – 0 = 10

When subtracting a number from itself, the answer is zero.

1 – 1 = 0	2 – 2 = 0
3 – 3 = 0	4 – 4 = 0
5 – 5 = 0	6 – 6 = 0
7 – 7 = 0	8 – 8 = 0
9 – 9 = 0	10 – 10 = 0

MATH+ Facts When Adding by 1

1 + 1 = 2	2 + 1 = 3
3 + 1 = 4	4 + 1 = 5
5 + 1 = 6	6 + 1 = 7
7 + 1 = 8	8 + 1 = 9
9 + 1 = 10	10 + 1 = 11

MATH+ Facts When Subtracting by 1

10 – 1 = 9	9 – 1 = 8
8 – 1 = 7	7 – 1 = 6
6 – 1 = 5	5 – 1 = 4
4 – 1 = 3	3 – 1 = 2
2 – 1 = 1	

MATH+ Step Up • Gr. 1–2 © 2011 Creative Teaching Press

Addition Fact Cards

$2 + 2 =$

$2 + 3 =$

$2 + 4 =$

$2 + 5 =$

$2 + 6 =$

$2 + 7 =$

$2 + 8 =$

$2 + 9 =$

$2 + 10 =$

$3 + 3 =$

Addition Fact Cards

$3 + 4 =$	$3 + 5 =$
$3 + 6 =$	$3 + 7 =$
$3 + 8 =$	$3 + 9 =$
$3 + 10 =$	$4 + 4 =$
$4 + 5 =$	$4 + 6 =$

Addition Fact Cards

$4 + 7 =$

$4 + 8 =$

$4 + 9 =$

$4 + 10 =$

$5 + 5 =$

$5 + 6 =$

$5 + 7 =$

$5 + 8 =$

$5 + 9 =$

$5 + 10 =$

Addition Fact Cards

6 + 6 =	6 + 7 =
6 + 8 =	6 + 9 =
6 + 10 =	7 + 7 =
7 + 8 =	7 + 9 =
7 + 10 =	8 + 8 =

Addition and Subtraction Fact Cards

$8 + 9 =$

$8 + 10 =$

$9 + 9 =$

$9 + 10 =$

$10 + 10 =$

$10 - 2 =$

$10 - 3 =$

$10 - 4 =$

$10 - 5 =$

$10 - 6 =$

Subtraction Fact Cards

$10 - 7 =$	$10 - 8 =$
$10 - 9 =$	$9 - 2 =$
$9 - 3 =$	$9 - 4 =$
$9 - 5 =$	$9 - 6 =$
$9 - 7 =$	$9 - 8 =$

Subtraction Fact Cards

8 − 2 =

8 − 3 =

8 − 4 =

8 − 5 =

8 − 6 =

8 − 7 =

7 − 2 =

7 − 3 =

7 − 4 =

7 − 5 =

Subtraction Fact Cards

$7 - 6 =$

$6 - 2 =$

$6 - 3 =$

$6 - 4 =$

$6 - 5 =$

$5 - 2 =$

$5 - 3 =$

$5 - 4 =$

$4 - 2 =$

$4 - 3 =$

Subtraction, Time, and Money Fact Cards

$$3 - 2 =$$

___, Monday, Tuesday

___, April, May

26¢	
75¢	68¢
$1.00	$2.15
12:30	6:00
Sunday March	11:00

MATH+ Step Up • Gr. 1–2 © 2011 Creative Teaching Press

Answer Key

PAGE 7

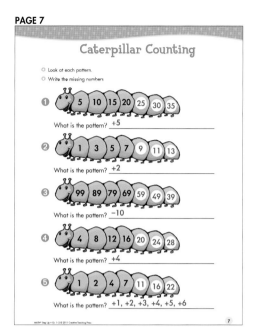

PAGE 8
1. 16
2. 32
3. 29
4. 72
5. 89
6. 43
7. 61
8. 56
9. 45
10. 91

PAGE 9
1. 36
2. 89
3. 62
4. 64
5. 28
6. 91
7. 49
8. 18

PAGE 10

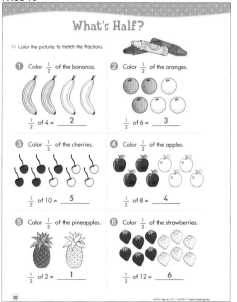

PAGE 11

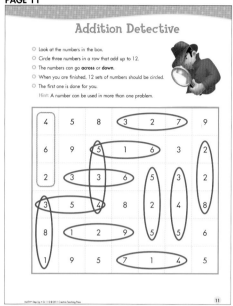

PAGE 12

Spider Web

- Cut out the number squares at the bottom of the page.
- Place the numbers in the spider web so that the sum of each row is 17.
- One number will be left over. What is it? __6__

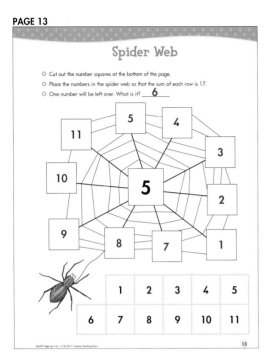

PAGE 15

1. 953
2. 359
3. 593
4. 641
5. 146
6. 461
7. 872
8. 278
9. 827

PAGE 16

Secret Subtraction

- There are 13 subtraction problems in this puzzle. The first one is done for you.
- Circle the other 12 problems.
- They can go **across** or **down**.

Hint: A number can be used in more than one problem.

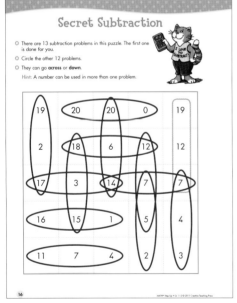

Plus and Minus Puzzler

- Look at each row of numbers.
- Write + or – in the circles to make two number sentences that are equal.

1. 3 (+) 5 = 9 (–) 1
2. 11 (–) 4 = 12 (–) 5
3. 6 (–) 4 = 8 (–) 6
4. 8 (+) 5 = 7 (+) 6
5. 10 (–) 5 = 2 (+) 3
6. 5 (+) 3 = 10 (–) 2
7. 6 (+) 6 = 9 (+) 3
8. 13 (–) 5 = 6 (+) 2
9. 11 (–) 2 = 3 (+) 6
10. 10 (–) 6 = 12 (–) 8
11. 7 (+) 3 = 2 (+) 8
12. 12 (–) 3 = 4 (+) 5

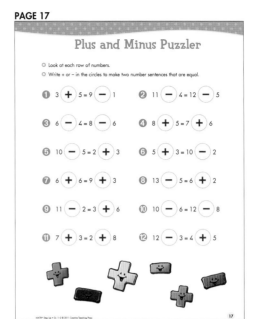

Play Ball!

- Subtract the numbers in each problem.
- Then circle the letters that belong to answers of 8 or less.
- Starting at the arrow, write the letters you circled in order on the lines below. The first one is done for you.

Riddle: **How did the player know the baseball was laughing?**

Answer:
IT WAS I N S T I T C H E S .

PAGE 19

Picnic Guest

- Help Adam Ant take three different paths to the picnic basket.
- Begin at each arrow and draw the path with a pencil.
- Then start with 19 and subtract the numbers along each path.
- Write your answers in the circles.

PAGE 20

1. 487
2. 268
3. 816
4. 900
5. 1,001
6. 806
7. 449
8. 356
9. 187
10. 914
11. 879
12. 473
13. 1,130
14. 1,200
15. 399
16. 795
17. 1,566
18. 1,220

PAGE 21

Passing the Time

- Solve each problem.
- Write the time.
- Then draw hands on the clock to match.

① The movie started at 3:00. It lasted 2 hours. What time did the movie end?
5:00

② Meg went to Kim's house at 11:30. She stayed for 3 hours. What time did Meg leave?
2:30

③ Lynn sleeps for 9 hours each night. She goes to bed at 9:00. What time does she get up?
6:00

④ Matt read for half an hour. He finished at 7:45. What time did Matt start reading?
7:15

⑤ Mr. Mays left home at 10:30. He returned 5 hours later. What time did he get home?
3:30

⑥ Mrs. Lum shopped for half an hour. She finished at 2:15. What time did she start shopping?
1:45

PAGE 22

1. 2:30
2. 8:15
3. 5:30
4. 9:00
5. 3:00
6. 5:15

PAGE 23

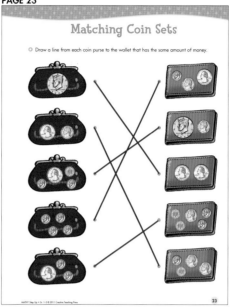

Matching Coin Sets

- Draw a line from each coin purse to the wallet that has the same amount of money.

PAGE 24

Money Match

- Fill in the bubble to show the correct answer.

① How much is this?   37¢ 60¢ 62¢

② How much is this?   40¢ 51¢ 61¢

③ How much is [ ] worth? $10 $1 $5

④ How much is this? $6.28 $10.00 $10.28

⑤ How much is this? $3.24
                    +$4.12 $7.36 $7.32 $1.12

⑥ Bob has 34¢. He spends 22¢ on
How much money is left?   46¢ 22¢ 12¢

PAGE 25

1. A balloon
2. 2 flags
3. An ice cream
4. A monkey
5. 20¢ more
6. 15¢ more
7. 3 balloons
8. A flag, a balloon, and an ice cream

PAGE 26
1. A bear and a yo-yo
2. A top and a drum
3. Sara bought a top. Kyle bought a yo-yo.
4. Nikki bought a ball. Brandon bought a car.
5. A top and a ball

PAGE 27
1. 50¢
2. 25¢
3. No change
4. 75¢
5. 40¢
6. 55¢
7. 85¢
8. 70¢

PAGE 28
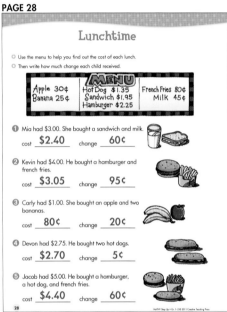

PAGE 29
1. 1 cup
2. 1 quart
3. 1 gallon
4. 1 pint
5. About 1 gallon

PAGE 30
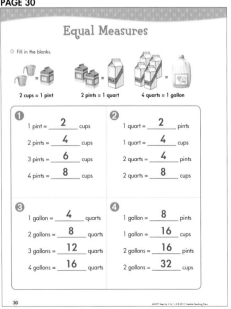

PAGE 31
1. 4
2. 12
3. more penguins
4. 10 altogether
5. 4 more
6. 2 more

PAGE 32
1. $1.00
2. $1.50
3. Room 4
4. $2.50
5. Room 2
6. 50¢
7. $1.50 more
8. $2.50 altogether

PAGE 33
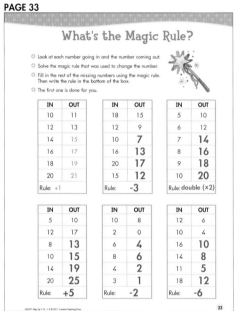

PAGE 34
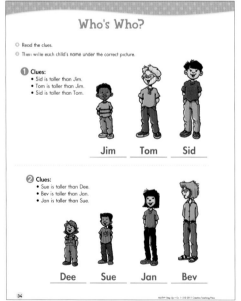

PAGE 35

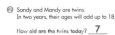

All in the Family

Solve the problems to find out everyone's age.

1. Jim is 3 years older than his sister Kim.
   Their ages add up to 13.

   How old is Jim? **8**
   How old is Kim? **5**

2. Sandy and Mandy are twins.
   In two years, their ages will add up to 18.

   How old are the twins today? **7**

3. Meg's mom is twice as old as Meg.
   Together, their ages add up to 60.

   How old is Meg? **20**
   How old is Meg's mom? **40**

4. Cory's dad is three times as old as Cory.
   Cory's grandfather is two times the age
   of Cory's dad.
   The ages of Cory, his dad, and his
   grandfather add up to 100.

   How old is Cory? **10**
   How old is Cory's dad? **30**
   How old is Cory's grandfather? **60**

35

PAGE 37
Possible answers: Yellow-purple-orange-blue-red; A-B-C-D-E
8 complete sets

PAGE 38
10 + 3 = 13

PAGE 39
12 < 13

PAGE 40
5 pairs
2 pairs

PAGE 41
6 sets
21 crayons

PAGE 42
4 more
8 more

PAGE 43
16 crayons
64 − 48 = 16

PAGE 44
20 > 4

PAGE 45
Possible answers: $\frac{2}{12}$; $\frac{1}{6}$

PAGE 46
1 set

PAGE 47
2 sets

PAGE 48
More than 50 crayons
Three sets of crayons are arranged in tallies of 5.

PAGE 49
9 + 8 = 17
24 crayons

PAGE 50
Possible answers: $\frac{2}{4}$; $\frac{1}{2}$

PAGE 51
$\frac{1}{4}$

Less than the fraction on page 50

PAGE 52
$\frac{1}{7}$

PAGE 55
Both tell time.
Possible answers: A stopwatch tells time in seconds, and a clock tells time in seconds, minutes, and hours.

PAGE 56
6 animals
Possible answers: They are in a race; The numbers help identify the animals when they race.

PAGE 57
It measures only up to 10 seconds.

PAGE 58
Snails move very slowly.

PAGE 59
5 animals

PAGE 60
12 inches

PAGE 61
4 animals
6 − 2 = 4

PAGE 62
19 more feet

PAGE 63
4, 5, and 6
2

PAGE 64
3 feet
Possible answers: You could add 100 three times (100 + 100 + 100 = 300);
You could add 3 one hundred times (3 + 3 + 3 + 3….= 300).

PAGE 65
The horse and the cheetah

PAGE 66
100 more yards

PAGE 67
The dog ran half the horse's distance.

PAGE 68
The bee stung the cheetah's nose.

PAGE 69
Yes
Possible answer: This was a 10-second race, and the partial picture of the stopwatch shows that only 9 seconds have gone by.

PAGE 70
Yes
Answers will vary.

PAGE 71

PAGE 72

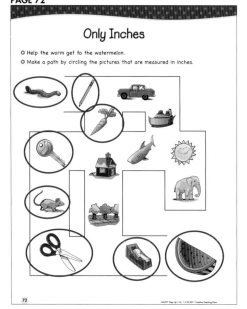

PAGE 73
Possible answer: Measuring lemonade

PAGE 74
He could jump in the pond of water behind him.

PAGE 75
Answers will vary.

PAGE 76
None

PAGE 77
3

PAGE 78
2

PAGE 79
2 more
4

PAGE 80
Possible answers: $\frac{4}{8}$ or $\frac{2}{4}$ or $\frac{1}{2}$

PAGE 81
8/8

PAGE 82
8 more

PAGE 83
2 cups

PAGE 84
4 cups

PAGE 85
Possible answer: You could add 2 four times (2 + 2 + 2 + 2 = 8)

PAGE 86
A half gallon

PAGE 87
1 gallon = 16 cups

PAGE 88
The cup jar

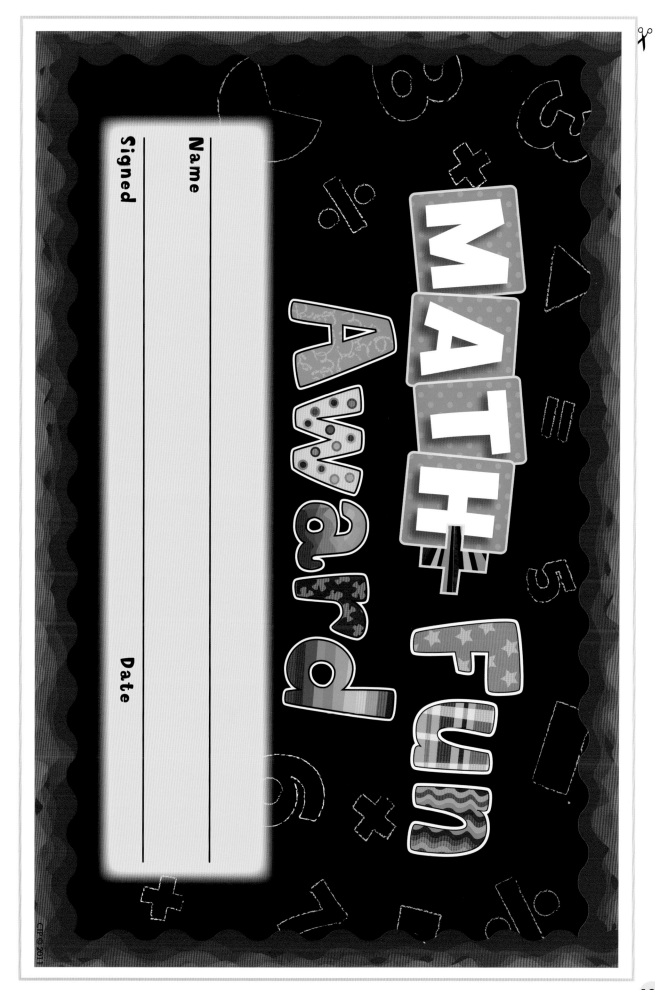

MATH Fun Award

Name _____

Signed _____ Date _____